The Drive of an Entrepreneur

7 Traits You Must Acquire

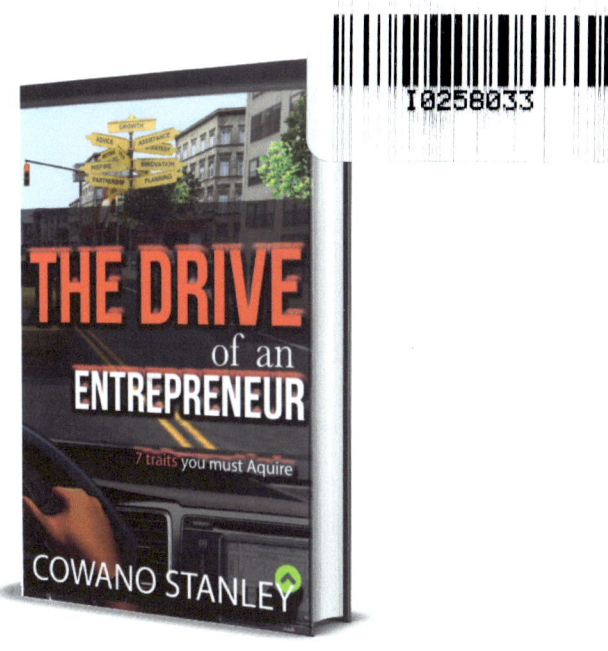

By CoWano Stanley

Copyright © 2020 By CoWano Stanley

All rights reserved. No part of this publication may be reproduced, distributed, or transmitted in any form or by any means including photocopying, recording, or other electronic or mechanical methods, without the prior written permission of the publisher, except in the case of brief quotations embodied in critical reviews and specific other noncommercial uses permitted by copyright laws.

Title: The Drive of an Entrepreneur
Subtitle: 7 Traits you Must Acquire
Author: CoWano Stanley
Publisher: CoWano Publishing, Inc.
ISBN: 978-0-578-84506-7
Cover Design: Kandie Enterprises, LLC
Web: www.Kandieenterprises.com
Facebook: www.facebook.com/kandieenterprises
Instagram: Instagram.com/kandieenterprises

TABLE OF CONTENTS

Acknowledgments………………………….Page 5

Chapter 1: Passion………………………...Page 7

    Keeping the Excitement

    Having Courage

    Empowerment

    Maintaining a Positive Attitude

Chapter 2: Determination……………….Page 14

    Believe in Yourself

    Calmness on the Journey

    Staying Focus

    Endurance During the Journey

    Being Competitive

Chapter 3: Creativity……………………..Page 24

    Being Flexible

    Strong Motivation

    Fearless

    Intense Curiosity

Chapter 4: Self-Starter…………………...Page 32

    Enthusiastic

    Loyalty is Earned

    Hard Work Pays Off

    Innovator

Chapter 5: Discipline……………………...Page 39

Staying Committed

Managing Your Time

Principle of Integrity

Strong Work Ethics

Chapter 6: Confidence……………….Page 46

Perfection Trap

Make the choice

Ignore the Negativity

Controlling the Mindset

Chapter 7: Strong people Skills……….Page 53

Communication and Listening

Patience with Others

Knowing Your Target Audience

Leadership

Conclusion……………………………...Page 60

About the Author…………………….Page 62

ACKNOWLEDGEMENT

Thanks to all those that supported and pre-order this book. I am profoundly grateful for your support.

-Gloria Abbott, Brooklyn Center, MN
-Debra Baker, Shine Bright Learning Center, Minneapolis, MN
-Jenae Brantley, IG:@brantleymobilebartending, Conyers, GA
-Eddie Brown, Minneapolis, MN
-Latrina Caldwell, IG:@author_latrina_c, Brooklyn Park, MN
-Monica Faulkner, Sistahs Beauty Supply, St. Cloud, MN.
-Jennifer Fontaine, Bowie, MD
-Dawona Harper, I Have Arrive, Minneapolis, MN
-Natasha Hunter, IG:@chocolatechicktees, Fort Worth, TX
-Brenda Yates-Hunter, Robbinsdale, MN
-Mardicia Johnson, Baytown, TX
-Kandie Martin, IG:@Kandie Enterprises, Riverdale, MN
-Lakeisha McGhee, IG:@lmcghee81, Brooklyn Center, MN.
-Danita Miller, Riverside, CA

-Nancy Montgomery, Shoreview, MN

-Melissa Newman, Minneapolis, MN

-Dorothy Nins, St. Paul, MN

-Patricia Pearson, Pearson Publishing LLC, Monmouth Junction, NJ.

-Rebecca Rabb, IG:@rabbuniverse, Plymouth, MN

-Isabell Rojas, IG:@rojaspublishing, Newburgh, NY

-LaShena Matthews, IG;@itsrecruitalina, Cumming, GA.

-Tiffany Smith, Tiffany By Design, LLC, Minneapolis, MN.

-Jerry Stanley (JJ), Raleigh, NC

-Jerry Ralph Stanley, Smackover, AR

-Venita Zeigler, Swift Management Solutions, Buffalo, NY

Chapter 1: Passion

Having passion is anything that gives you the drive needed to keep the excitement of what it is that you are passionate about. Being an entrepreneur, you need to be passionate about what it is you are doing. Passion gives you a reason to want to keep learning and pushing towards the mastery of your passion. Your passion will challenge you in areas that you may not be comfortable in but will also bring the best of your gift out. Usually, you find out that your gift is your passion. It is something you like doing without even thinking twice about it. *A man's gift will make room for him & bring him before great men (Proverbs 18:16 KJV)*. So, in other words, when you use your gift that within you, it will open doors and give you access to great important people. It will also put you in a position that your finances will come looking for and you will not have to chase it. There are many characteristics that come with having passion. The passion that you have whether that is a product or service will give you your customers the excitement for what you are offering. Always, make sure your customers see the passion in you. As an entrepreneur, every day is not going to be a great day, but you can find a way to still stay passionate.

Your passion comes from within. So, make sure you have the passion.

Keeping the Excitement

Being able to keep excitement when it comes to your passion is a job within itself. When it comes to excitement it takes a mindset of control to make sure you still have the drive to stay excited about your passion. There will be times when you do not have the excitement about your passion. Things will come up along the way to get you sidetracked off the focus. One way to make sure you keep the excitement is by remembering your WHY. Why are you doing what you are doing? Is it your passion? If you write your WHY down somewhere where you are always seeing it, it will keep you excited. Another way to stay excited about your passion is by staying organized. If you stay organized within a way that keeps things in an orderly fashion and an agenda, then you will stay excited. One more way to stay excited about your passion as an entrepreneur is by adding a little mediation to your day every day before you get started with your day or before your duties. So always work on and make sure you are staying excited about your passion. Remember if you keep the excitement for your passion as an entrepreneur then others will recognize it as well. If you are excited others will be excited. If you are interested in learning more about things that tie into this I write on or coach about please go www.cowanostanley.com.

Having Courage

Now, courage is one that is a development that is needed. As an entrepreneur, you cannot be afraid to step out. If you allow fear to step in front of you then you will miss out on opportunities that may be available for you in the future. Having the courage to step out and be an entrepreneur is a big step in the first place. So be proud of yourself that you have the courage to become or be an entrepreneur. It takes courage to even make that decision. To have courage is also believing in yourself that you can do it, despite any challenges that may come along. I remember there were times years ago that I was afraid to even speak in front of a crowd of more than 25. But as I began to become into who I knew I was and who is I was (God-fearing woman) and then replaced that with courage. Now do not get me wrong there are times when new opportunities or situations may come up that I may be a little nervous about doing. However, being a little nervous is okay but I have strong courage to do what I love to do. When you are doing what you love, you push through and pass the fear and have that courage. Sometimes with business, you will need to have the courage and be able to make a quit decision, so you do not lose out on an opportunity that is right there in front of you. So, you have no time to be fearful at that moment. A quick decision will need to be made. So, if you do not have any courage, you need to get some

Empowerment

When it comes to empowerment, you must bold and be outspoken. As you are the expert that your followers or future clients are looking to. You need to be able to see and have a vision of where you are going. In empowering yourself, you must give people the motivation or inspiration that they need to go forward or to keep pushing. But always keeping yourself empowered during coaching and teaching others. When you are loving what you do as an entrepreneur or if you are a beginning entrepreneur the empowering will come with growth and maturity. Another thing with empowerment you must keep learning yourself by investing in yourself. For example, you can listen to motivational speakers such as Les Brown or Eric Thomas. You can buy courses that help you to grow within yourself. Time is an investment as well. Whatever it is that will help you to stay motivated and inspire within do it. What's inside of you will come out. So, what you are learning will start to show through your coaching or teaching or services. When empowering others you cannot be afraid. As I spoke in the previous topic about courage, you need to step outside your comfort zone. Once you can do that then you can do anything. Empowerment comes from knowing who you are and believing what is in you and give that to others. So about 2 weeks ago I was speaking with a high school friend on the phone. She stated to me that I have always inspired her. She said that I help inspired her in a certain situation in high school she was dealing at the time and she will never forget. To my surprise, I did not even know that I had inspired her, nor did I remember at that moment. So, my point is that you never know who will help empower with what is in you to give.

Positive Attitude

Having a positive attitude is always one thing that will take work and a mindset to keep. As an entrepreneur, there will be times when you may not feel like having a positive attitude because something may have gone wrong that with your business such as business was slow that day, sales were low, no clients or just something personal. You may have even gotten some family bad news. However, find a way to turn that negative attitude into a positive attitude. So, the thing you will need to do is learn what will help you to get or stay in a positive attitude. Maybe it will be some uplifting music, or some audio of positive words given. Whatever it is, just make sure you learn some different mediation ways to get you in a positive attitude along the way. As an entrepreneur, this is a trait that must be carried. An entrepreneur's job is never to give up or quit because of the journey of changes that you will go through. Not to mention having a positive attitude goes right along with being able to keep the passion for your business as an entrepreneur. So, both go hand and hand. As a matter of fact, there has been plenty of times where my attitude was not in a positive way. Yes me. It happens to us all; it is a part of life experiences and journey. We all have a path that we must go through on our own, but it is all a part of growing and adjusting to changing the thought process along the way to positive. If you learn to keep a positive attitude in a way that keeps you pushing and a passion for what you are doing, then you are growing as you should.

Chapter 2: Determination

Having determination is a trait that is well needed during pursuing entrepreneurship or if you are already an entrepreneur. If you do not have determination as an entrepreneur, you will not last long as an entrepreneur. You will need determination on the journey when; no one will believe in what you are doing, no one sees your vision, no money is not coming in regularly as an entrepreneur, you have made a bad investment for building your business, when you are frustrated and in life to keep going you will need determination. Determination will help you accomplish your goals. It will help remind you why you started that business. Determination will push you to success. So, as you can see determination is a driven trait that will keep you moving forward with your goals and not take no for an answer. When you are driven and determined to hit the goals you have set, you are unstoppable. Stay looking ahead. Your determination will take you further than you can ever imagine. So, if you are a determined new entrepreneur, stay determined and keep going no matter what obstacles you will face on your path. If you are already an entrepreneur, then do not stop being determined. You continue to grind hard and accomplish those goals. Dreams become goals and goals become reality. That determination that you have will pay off. Determination comes in many different forms of characteristics. In this chapter, you will find more characteristics that break down determination.

Believe in yourself

Believing in yourself is a task that only you can do for yourself. If you do not believe in yourself, who will? It all starts with you first. You are the one that must believe in you, in order to become what you desire to become. If you want to be an entrepreneur, you most definitely need to believe in you. Whatever the dreams or goals you have, it is going to take the first step on your part by believing in yourself. When people see that you believe in your goals or dreams, then they will believe in you. Now let me say this, do not get caught up in thinking everyone will believe in you or your goals. Just keep believing in yourself and pushing forward on your goals. When you believe in yourself, you learn more about what your abilities and challenges are. You also learn what your strengths and weakness are that you may not have recognized before. There will be moments when you are given a vision by God about something to do and it seems impossible, but you know you need to do it. It will take everything in you for you to believe in that vision and not worry about who will believe in it with you or not. Just ask God for guidance and keep pushing towards the goal. You can do anything you put your mind to. Everything is not going to be easy. If it was easy everyone will be doing it. So just stay believing in yourself. As an entrepreneur, it is a must to believe in you. For more information please go to www.cowanostanley.com.

Calmness on the Journey

Being calm is a state of mind that will allow you to stay in a free mindset. Calmness as an entrepreneur will be needed because it will help you navigate through the challenges that will come. For those of you that are an entrepreneur you know and understand what I am talking about. If you are interested in being an entrepreneur, you will need to have this trait. You will need to stay level-headed as an entrepreneur through some of the ups and downs in your business. Sometimes you may just have to take a deep breath and relax just to stay calm if you find yourself getting frustrated and overwhelmed. Of course, having calmness will take some practice to make a habit of doing. Just like you have other habits (good or bad), this is one that you want to become a habit in a positive way. Do not allow yourself to panic during challenges that will come your way for your business. You will need to find ways to help you to stay calm to be able to keep pushing forward. Getting rid of any anxiety will help along the way. Having anxiety is a whole different topic or book, LOL. I want you to figure out the ways that you stay calm and use it at any given time in life and as an entrepreneur. Meditation is always a good way to be able to relax your mind and find calmness. The meditation will help you find a way to keep your mindset in a good space as well as your thoughts. We know the thoughts are enormously powerful and if our thoughts are not good then it will rub off on our business. Remember energy is everything. So be mindful and recognize when frustration or anxiety is coming about so that you can find a way to stay calm.

Staying Focus

Staying focus is one that we all have a challenge with at times. There are many things that can get in our way to get us out focused. Not that we intentionally try to be out focused but sometimes life happens. As an entrepreneur, many of you may have spouses and children and your businesses to run. So sometimes these things may get in the way of one another. But you must find a way to be able to stay focused on what your goal is or completing assignments. A good way to stay focused is by setting up and organizing a balance between everything to make sure you stay focus. One of the things that I do is write down everything that needs to be done for the next day, prior to the next day. That way I do not get off track of the things that need to be done for that day. I have a coach that says, "If it's not on my schedule, it does not exist". Yes, sometimes it may not go exactly the way that I want it to go but at least I have an idea of what needs to be done in a prioritizing order. One of the ways I stay focused is by getting up early and starting my day. Starting early will help you get some of those things on your list out of the way early. As an entrepreneur make sure you are always getting things done related to your business. And of course, your family. This way you are staying connected with your business, as well as your family time. Another way and staying focused is by writing down what things are wasting your time and maybe allocate that to an assistant. Yes, you can do a virtual assistant. Make sure you are putting your energy and time into the things that are important first in order to stay focused. You will find that some of that busy work can be given to someone else to do or just do not need it. There are many things we all can stop doing that are wasting our time and energy. Yes, taking a break sometimes is okay, just do not get unfocused to long on your break.

Endurance During the Journey

Endurance is one that many along the journey will throw in the towel. The reason being is because endurance you must be able to stand through some challenges even though it may be long and hard work. However, with endurance, you will see the results in the end if you just stick through it. You will need the endurance to achieve some goals that you have set for yourself. With endurance, you are going to have to set your mind to say no matter what I will go through this and get through it. When I first step outside of my comfort zone and started my cleaning business, I did not have all the answers. I learned a lot and went through a lot as I went. There were times when I said to myself that I am going to just put this business on pause. But as I got my thoughts together, I knew that was not the answer to giving up or putting my business on pause. So, I made a conscious decision that I was not toweling in the towel. Endurance is not an easy task to go through however it is worth it. Sometimes the road to endurance on the journey will get difficult but you still must withstand it in order to receive the end results. This is your race no one else. Endurance will help you push through growing pains and learn how to tackle bigger goals that are ahead. As an entrepreneur wanting to go to the next level will take some endurance, it will give you the strength that you need for the next level. You cannot get to the next level if you cannot get to the level that you are on. Each level will consist of new endurance. So, the test and trial as an entrepreneur will come on all levels. So, if you want to be an entrepreneur be prepared and ready to carry endurance. There are times when you will need endurance especially when business is not going well. You will need to know how to navigate and push yourself through the challenge, come up with ideas to get your business where you want it to be.

Being Competitive

When it comes to being competitive it doesn't always mean that you are competing with other people, but you are competing against yourself; such as you need to stretch yourself more to push yourself to the next level. Some people will review competitive as an obstacle. But others will see it as an opportunity. Which way do you see it? As an entrepreneur, I said both, it is an obstacle in a positive way because it helps build myself up and my business. Obstacles will come along the way and try to stop you. They are designed to slow you down and, in some cases, stop you. As the saying goes, "We are our own worst enemy", so in other words, we are our biggest competitor and critic. We will talk ourselves out of a great opportunity that seems impossible, but nothing is impossible. You can do anything that you put your mind to. Competitiveness is a good thing because it helps you push yourself to a strength that you never thought you can do. As an entrepreneur or if you are starting to become an entrepreneur never let what someone else is doing keeps you from doing what you want to do even if it is the same business. We all are unique in our own ways. So, no matter what business you choose to do, move forward doing it or push yourself to do more to grow your business.

Never stop learning and growing within yourself in your business because of competitiveness. Remember competitive is positive because it will help push you outside of your comfort zone.

Chapter 3: Creativity

Being able to have some creativity as a trait as an entrepreneur is especially important. With creativity, you must be able to come up with or develop new ideas that may help with your business. When problems or situations come up in your business you will need to have some solutions. In life, whether it has personal or business, there are always problems that just need a solution. When you have that creativity, you think outside the box. You do not think about things based on the norm or tradition. Being creative as an entrepreneur, you will not feel bad by changing things that need to be changed. There will be times when you have been doing something in your business for so long that no longer works that way. You will have to be open-minded and make changes. You cannot get caught up and stay stagnant. You must find and implement new ways and ideas for your business. Never feel bad about making some adjustments and changes to your business. There will be times when things are out of your control such as the Pandemic caused by the Corona Virus. A lot of businesses are hurting and even going out of business. Right now, I am quite sure businesses are focused on coming up with different ways to do things due to the pandemic. So as a business owner being creative is necessary. Occasionally it is okay to get some constructive criticism from your team as well as your customers to see what changes can be made. If you are overthinking at times just take a mental break and come back to it later. But just keep an open mind.

Being Flexible

As an entrepreneur, you need to have some flexibility when it comes to your schedule. Flexible is a great characteristic of creativity. They go hand and hand. Your schedule will often be based on your business. There will be times when you need to adjust your schedule or change some things around to be flexible. Whether you are a full-time entrepreneur or part-time entrepreneur flexibility is always needed. Whatever industry your business is in you need to stay on top of the changes that will come so you know how to make the changes and adjustments. Sometimes opportunities will come your way and it will consist of making some adjustments to your schedule. If you are not flexible you can lose that opportunity that is at the door. Not only do you need to be flexible, but your business needs to be flexible. Especially in today's time, many businesses are very flexible due to the technology that we have available. As a business owner and entrepreneur, I am always flexible. Let us not forget that your mindset needs to be flexible and open-minded to make changes. As an entrepreneur, there will be many things you will not have much control over as far as some of the changes that you may have to be flexible with. When being an entrepreneur many things are changing, and you will need to learn how to adapt to some of the flexible changes. Do not get bent out of shape when you must make changes just write out the pros and cons and make the adjustments needed.

Strong Motivation

When it comes to strong motivation you do not only need self-motivation for yourself but also motivation for your clients or customers. Having strong motivation will help you as an entrepreneur to implement new ideas in your business. Your motivations will keep you on your toes to better in areas of your business. You must be able to motivate yourself every day in order to stay positive and uplifting. If you want your business to grow or if you want to make sure your customers and clients are happy you need to make sure you have strong motivation. If you are not motivated, then your business nor your customers and clients will be motivated. Your energy is everything. You must be able to push through no matter what the obstacles and situations are. Every day will be a challenge for you and your business. But you must find a way to stay motivated even when you do not feel like it. Every day is not going to be a great day when it comes to your business but if you stay motivated within yourself you will be simply fine. Everyday practice with words of affirmations and meditation that will help you to stay motivated. How you wake up to start your day every day can determine how your day will go and how your motivation will be for that day.

So, do not let anything start your day off with bad energy or a bad mindset. You set your day by starting with the great motivation words and energy so that today will be a great day even if it is not it keeps you in a positive mindset of having a great positive day.

Fearless

Are you a Fearless person? One of the things that set other successful entrepreneurs apart is them being fearless. Being a business owner or entrepreneur most problems that come along with business is not new. It is how you face those problems that come up and finding solutions to deal with them. Being fearless means to be able to not allow fear to stop you from moving forward and handling problems in a way where the problem does not handle you. Fearless people are confident within themselves that does not keep them stagnant from making decisions. When you are fearless you do not mind taking risks. In entrepreneurship, you will need to be fearless because there will be many times when you must make decisions that are unexpected. One quote that I love by Kobe Bryant is "If you are afraid to fail then you probably will fail". You cannot be afraid of what the outcomes may be in a situation. Each situation in our life will only help us to become better. You are what you believe you are. As an entrepreneur when you are fearless you are not afraid to speak up when necessary of having a different opinion. When you are fearless you do not worry about what other people think of you. When you are fearless you are bold and real. And this is not in a negative way but in a way that you know what you mean, and you know what you said you stand for what you stand for. So being fearless is a good trait to have as an entrepreneur because you are not afraid to go forth with doing something different from others. For more additional information go to www.cowanostanley.com.

Intense curiosity

As an entrepreneur do you have an intense curiosity. Do you ask a lot of questions when you do not know the answer to? Do you listen well? Well with these questions as an entrepreneur you have curiosity. It is good to ask questions when you do not know the answer to them. The only dumb question is the one that you do not ask. If you are a new entrepreneur, they are going to be plenty of things that you must learn along the way and it is a good time to start asking those questions from experienced entrepreneurs. Experienced entrepreneurs and other business owners will be glad to give you the information that you do not know. Never think anything is wrong with asking questions that you do not know the answer to. This is the way that you will be able to learn and grow. When it comes to curiosity you cannot be afraid to say you do not know. So anytime their questions or answers you need to know as an entrepreneur feel free to always seek and search from others. When becoming a new entrepreneur, you are going to need curiosity such as searching the industry that you are trying to be in. As you search the industry that you are trying to be in, look for what things your customers and business may need. So, the more information and knowledge that you get regarding your industry the better and easier things will be along the way. So never let anyone make you feel like your curiosity is the meaning of insecurity because it is not.

Chapter 4: Self-Starter

Are you a person that has that go-getter attitude/behavior? Are you a person that goes ahead and does things without always needing the direction on what to do? Are you a macro manage person? If that is, you then you are a self-starter. Self-starter is what a lot of entrepreneurs must have in starting their own business adventure. When being an entrepreneur you will not always have the answers right away. Some things will be trial and error or learning on your own. Some things you will need to know as you travel on the journey of being an entrepreneur. As a self-starter, you will need to make some decisions on your own. Self-starters are exceptionally good at being entrepreneurs because they like taking the initiative. As a self-starter, you cannot rely on others to make decisions. If you are a self-starter, you will navigate your way through what is needed to get to where you want to go. When I step outside of being a full-time entrepreneur, I had to research and learn how a lot. But because I was a self-starter, I trusted the process and gained a lot along the way. If you are a new entrepreneur, you may have to start off small with some things in your business. But that okay you are just getting started. As you build your business you will figure out what works and does not work. Being a self-starter is a plus as an entrepreneur. So, keep it up!

Enthusiastic

When being a self-starter, you most definitely need to have enthusiasm. When having enthusiasm, do you have it for your business or your passion? Well if not you need it as an entrepreneur. If you are not enthusiastic about your passion or your business, then no one else will be. I think enthusiasm is one of the most powerful traits to have for an entrepreneur. Having enthusiastic Is important and vital to have in order to be a successful entrepreneur. For example, if your car has no fuel in it, then your car cannot move. So, therefore, if you do not have much energy and enthusiasm as an entrepreneur your business will go nowhere. Being excited about your business as an entrepreneur should be especially important to you. You should always want to bring forth positive, great, firing energy. I stated before there will be ups and downs in your business. But you must find a way to stay fired up, excited, and enthusiastic about your business. Whatever goals and dreams that you want to accomplish, the enthusiastic in you will make sure you get it done. Here's a great quote by Gordon Parks, the first African American Photographer for Life and Vogue magazine said, "Enthusiasm is the electricity of life. How do you get it? You act enthusiastic until it becomes a habit." No one can give you the enthusiasm that you need but you. Every day that you work on your business or your passion you should be enthusiastic about it as if you were just starting it. This would give you the push that you need to keep working on your business or passion despite any situation that is going on.

Loyalty is Earned

As a self-starter of your business, when it comes to loyalty you must be loyal with yourself and your business as well as your customers and clients. Having loyalty will give you a strong foundation for your business. Even as your business grows and you must build a team your employees are only going to be loyal to you as you are loyal to them. So, having some loyalty will come in all different ways that you would need for your business. It only takes one of them to fall through for everything to fall through. So, it is your responsibility as an entrepreneur to make sure your loyalty is true all the way across the board. No matter what business you are in you will always need loyalty from your customers and clients because they will be a big part of your business being successful. If you have no customers and clients, you have no business. Being an entrepreneur, you need to make sure that you make your customers and clients a priority. One thing that helps build loyalty with your customers and clients is getting feedback from your customers or clients to see what their reviews are of your business. Another way in building customer loyalty is by making sure you have excellent customer service. Many of us have been to plenty of places where the customer service was so horrible. As a customer what do we do, we do not go back to that place again. Another one is to build customer loyalty by building a relationship with the community where your business is, even on social media. So, as you can see there are many ways to build loyalty but most importantly is to be loyal to yourself and your business and treat your business as a priority.

Hard work pays off

When starting a business, you must be a hard worker. Are you hard working when it comes to your business or even your personal life? Do you put a lot of energy into making sure something gets done and it is worked out? If the answer is yes, then you played a vital part in being hard-working. Do you do just enough to get things done or do you go above and beyond? Well, hard-working people go above and beyond and do more than what is required & needed to get the job done. Let us take me as an example. I know without a doubt that I am a very hard-working individual, entrepreneur, mother, business owner, & author. I do my best to make sure I go above and do more than what is needed so that I can get the best out of what I am doing and get great results. This is a skill or trait that I have always had in me as I grew up and to this day I still put in a lot of hard work. As an entrepreneur and business owner, you will need to put in a lot of hard work and time in order to be successful in your business. Nothing will come easy as you travel on the journey of being an entrepreneur. Although there will be times it feels like you are putting in more hard work and not seeing any results, but results will always show up in due time. The hard work and time that you invest will come forth. So never give up putting in the hard work. For more information please go to www.cowanostanley.com.

Innovator

When becoming an entrepreneur and being a self-starter of your business, you must be an innovator. When being an innovator you are always going to be on the lookout for new business changes etc. These may be things that will make your business better or easier. With me, I am always looking for new apps and software that will be beneficial to my business. Many businesses have adjusted and made changes when it comes to technology. With the times that we live in now a lot of the business may do things such as automatic business emails sent out to you. This means the business owner does not necessarily have to be sitting in front of a computer to send an email out, the system is set up to automatically send to its subscribed customers. Let us take this as an example; Samsung or Apple both companies are innovators because they find new ways to make their phones & laptops better than the last phone or laptop every year. So, you or your team must be on the lookout for the market that you are in for any new or updated changes that need to be done. And when it comes to some of the changes as an innovator you need to be able to find a solution to the changes. Just like any other business where the software or system needs a change and for you to stay ahead of the game you need to make the changes. So being an innovator is a great trait to have as an entrepreneur because it keeps you ahead of what is to come. So as a new or already entrepreneur continues to be or adapt to be an innovator to better your business or make an easier way or doing some things.

Chapter 5: Discipline

As an entrepreneur discipline is one that is very much needed no matter what. When you are disciplined as an entrepreneur you are responsible and accountable for yourself and everything that needs to be done. No one is there to tell you what and when to do it. If you do not have discipline already you will need to acquire this. Discipline is not always easy to follow. You must be strict with yourself at times in order to make sure you are getting things done and putting in the work needed for your business. Even when things come up at the last minute you are the one that must get the job done. So, are you disciplined? Being discipline will consist of you having consistency. Having consistency in your business will help keep your business in order. Being discipline will also help lead you to success. When you have discipline, you are showing responsibility. There are plenty of parts in your business that you must be disciplined with. Look it is not a walk in a park being an entrepreneur. However, I will not change being an entrepreneur because I love what I do. Who wants to deal with the boss of a business that is not responsible? Exactly I sure do not. But believe it or not, there are some entrepreneurs that are not disciplined enough when it comes to their business.

Which is probably why they will not last long in their business. So, make sure that you are a person that is disciplined.

Staying Committed

When staying committed as an entrepreneur can sometimes get tired along the way before getting to the finish line. This is due to the unknown and frustration. When you are an entrepreneur you must stay the course. Things will be uncertain at times because you are working for yourself. Putting in the work that is needed to grow your business will come at the right time if you stay committed to the goal and process. Giving up or quitting should not be an option. If something is not working, then find a way to approach the situation and fix it. It is better to try to do something different then to throw in the towel. Also, in order to stay committed as an entrepreneur, you must be passionate about what it is you are doing. If you are not passionate about what you are doing and you do not stay committed, then things will be short-lived. Being an entrepreneur, the process will take hard work. The frustration comes due to some of the experiences and challenges that will come as an entrepreneur. So, make sure you are passionate about your business & do not let hardship get you off track and stay committed. Staying committed to something is a way of being disciplined as we previously stated in the topic prior. If you find yourself getting to the point of not being committed to your business, then find a way to get back on track to your dream or goal. So, keep pushing and moving forward and stay committed to what you are doing so that you do see the end results that you have set. For more valuable information please check out www.cowanostanley.com.

Managing your Time

Now, are you managing your time wisely? Do you have things organized in a way to manage your time? Well, many will find themselves not managing their time wisely the way it needs to be when it comes to their business. Especially if you have multiple businesses that you run. When managing your time as an entrepreneur one thing I do is write down the things that have to be completed for the next day. This will give you a sense of how much is needed for your business, family & personal. You must find ways to balance all of this. There will be plenty of times where more time will be on business than family etc. As an entrepreneur, you will sometime be putting in more hours than a normal eight to five job. But this is to get your business where you want it. Another tip that can be done to manage time is by scheduling and organizing appointments and entering it on your calendar. This will keep your stuff organized. When scheduling also makes sure that you put a time frame on each item. Another way to manage your time is by prioritizing your list of to do. Putting the most important to the least important can keep things in order also. One last good way to manage your time as an entrepreneur is by finding ways to automate your business. With all the technology we have in place currently there are many software tools and apps. that you can put in place to help some of your day-to-day business needs. Some examples to automate your business are emails and data that need to be sent out and hiring a virtual assistant for online duties you need to be done (you can find them unbelievably cheap and reasonable). So, if you try some of the things you can manage your time well as an entrepreneur.

Principle of Integrity

What does integrity mean to you as an entrepreneur? What does it mean to you in life? Well, integrity is when you do the right thing because it is the right thing to do. Even if people do not like the fact that you have integrity about yourself, you keep your integrity. As an entrepreneur, you must be unique and true to yourself. If you are a leader in business, you want to make sure that you have integrity about yourself because this is where your respect will come in place. Integrity in business is particularly important. Integrity also leads to success. There is a quote that says, "What you put out will come back to you." So, if you put out doing the right thing good seeds will come back to you. What you are speaking to others make sure you are walking it as well. Never let what others are doing (especially if it does not feel right) get you outside of what you believe is right to do or it can make you lose your integrity. Never lose your truth. Do not even let fear take you off track of your integrity. Integrity is one principle that I love having. You must build your business so that people know that you have integrity about yourself. Such as keeping commitments, speaking the truth, and treating people right. If you are an entrepreneur and have a team, your team will follow your ways of having integrity also. If you are wanting to become an entrepreneur, make sure you have integrity about yourself.

Strong Work Ethics

Having a strong work ethic is a must trait to have as an entrepreneur. You must put in lots of work and hours as an entrepreneur if you want success with your business. If you do not have it, you will fail. A strong work ethic will consist of you having passion, energy, and commitment. As an entrepreneur, you need to come with everything within you to keep pushing forth of your business. Will you be tired some days? Yes. Will you get frustrated some days? Yes. Will you get stuck some days? Yes. However, if you are dedicated to reaching your goal you need to keep going and putting in the work. When having a strong work ethic, you also need to be consistent. Stay consistent with your business and keep repeating and repeating and repeating. Eventually what you are sowing will grow. With having a strong work ethic, you will be driven to push through the obstacle. As stated, before if you have a passion for what you are doing your work ethic will automatically be strong. Let us make it clear you cannot be lazy with your business. So if you see you are getting lazy and not having any strong work ethic, you may need to re-evaluate if what you are doing is the right business or you need to find a way to get you back focused on your business. So, with a strong work ethic, it has a lot of qualities in one that you need in order to have a strong work ethic. Just check yourself to see what you are missing within yourself if you see your work ethic is not strong.

Chapter 6: Confidence

Another great trait that is needed as an entrepreneur is having confidence. Confidence is one that you must believe in yourself that you can do. Confidence is something that comes from within. No one can give you the confidence that you need for your business or in life but you. You are the one that must have confidence and believe in your products and services that you offered for your business. If you have the confidence that is needed, and everyone sees that then they will have confidence in it. So, make sure as an entrepreneur that you have the confidence that is needed when you start your business. Confidence is gained and build up. One thing confidence does is helps your mental health. We know that mental health is particularly important. When you have confidence, you are open to opportunities that come your way. With confidence, people will believe in your product or services. With confidence, you do not sit around waiting on others to make the decisions. If you are reading this and you are a new entrepreneur or even current entrepreneur, taking the steps to be your boss is much confidence. The more you continue to push for your goals and accomplish them the more your confidence will grow. So, continue to build your confidence no matter what.

Your growth in your career, business, and personal life. The confidence will help Moving forward in this chapter we will talk about many other characteristics that will tie into confidence.

Perfection trap

One of the things that tie into confidence is being a perfectionist trap person. As an entrepreneur, you want to be perfect in everything you do in your business. You want to make sure things are set up right and put outright. Yes, things will go wrong along the way in your business, and mistakes will happen as an entrepreneur, however you try to do everything as perfectly as possible. You want to make sure you are giving the customers the best service & products. So, although you may be a perfection trap person as an entrepreneur it is the confidence in you that allows you to want to do things as perfect as you can get them. If you do not put too much pressure on yourself and just do the best you can do, having a perfection trap behavior is not such a bad thing to have as an entrepreneur. If you see yourself get into the place where you have a meltdown because it is not as perfect as you want it to be, take a break and come back to it later. This way you do not overwhelm yourself of being stuck if it is not perfect. Being a perfectionist trap, this can be a good characteristic because it pushes you to think outside of the box and think of other great ways to make something work. A perfectionist trap would not give up until it is right. Perfectionist trap will put in a lot of work and time. So, if you manage this in a way to where it has not a hindrance to you, you will be fine with this being a perfection trap.

Make the choice

When being an entrepreneur or becoming an entrepreneur, making choices are going to be a lot of things that you must do. In life, many choices you will have to make. Some choices that you make will have to be right on the spot and some will be something that you have to think about. As an entrepreneur, you will have to take many risks and make choices and decisions. You will not always know if you are making the right choice or decision or not because some of the things that you go through as an entrepreneur will be trial and error. As I stated before. Every entrepreneur's choices that they have made have been based on trial and error. Not everyone's situation is going to be the same. There are many different stories and books on being an entrepreneur and making choices. But everyone's story of their journey will be a little different from the last person. Do not beat yourself up on some of the choices that you may have to made or will make in your business. If you do not make the choices how would you know if the choice was right or wrong? The one thing that I never regret is making the choice to become an entrepreneur. This is one of the best decisions I have made in my life. So, if you are looking to become an entrepreneur, just know that this can be one of the best decisions that you will make. For more information on making choices go to www.cowanostanley.com.

Ignore the negativity

One of the main things you must do is make sure that you ignore all negativity. You cannot allow negative things or people to come in your thoughts because it would disrupt your attitude about our entrepreneurship. There are going to be people that say you should not be an entrepreneur, or they may even say that your product or service is not good. However, you cannot let the negativity get you off track from what is your goal and vision is for you. There will be times when you may question your business and negativity will creep in because things are not going the way that you wanted your business to go. But you cannot let that get you off track either. Only you know the vision and goal that you have sent out for your business. Anything worth having is not going to be easy. So, some challenges will come along the way as an entrepreneur. Try and channel yourself to thinking of things positively in order to maintain the mindset of not having negativity interrupt what you got going on. Having affirmations and positive words set by you each day will help you keep a positive attitude as an entrepreneur. Also do not worry about the opinions of what others think of you. You cannot put yourself with the toxic negative energy of people who say you should not be an entrepreneur, or you cannot be an entrepreneur. As it is said, ignore the haters you are doing something that they are not.

Controlling your Mindset

One of the things that's huge is that you must control your mindset because there are many things that will keep you from focusing on what you need to be doing. As an entrepreneur, you must keep control over what comes to you. You must control your emotions, your thoughts, actions, and energy. If your mindset is not in the right space to be focused on your business, then your energy will also be off. Your energy is everything. If you do not think positively about your business things will be off. I said it before you are what you think you are. It does not take much for your mindset to be in a different space to where things will be off with yourself and your business. You must find ways to control your mindset in a way that you are always ready, so you do not have to get ready. The one thing about emotions is if your emotions are not good then they can have you making decisions that send you in a different direction opposite of your vision and goal. One thing you can do to stay focused on controlling your mindset is writing a list of things that you need to stay focused on such as; what your vision is, what's your daily goals, your monthly goals, or yearly goals for your business. Do not allow any distractions to come into your circle or space. Stay around positive, motivational, and inspiring people. This will also help with making sure your mindset is in a good space. Another thing that can help you keep your mindset in a good space is by reading or listening to audio from motivational speakers and praying/meditating. So, if you can learn to control what comes in and out of your mindset then you will do great as being an entrepreneur and staying focused on your end results and goals.

Chapter 7: Strong People Skills

When you become an entrepreneur or if you're already an entrepreneur you will need to develop strong people skills because the majority of you may be offering a product and service that will have to deal with people. Having strong people skill is very essential to your business. Having people skills, you will need to be able to empathize with people and understand them. One of the things that I love about myself is being able to inspire others, which is also a people skill. This comes naturally to me. Another way to be able to have strong people skills is being able to relate to them. Just like other characteristics and traits in this book that I have listed and talked about, having people skills is a particularly important trait. If your strong people skills are not that good you can always practice working on them and read up on things that will help develop the skill as you become an entrepreneur. There are many tools and exercises you can do to help build your people skills. As you read this chapter you will see some of the characteristics that consist of having people skills. This is an ongoing trait that must be practiced daily to make a habit of doing it. Believe me when I say everyone is not going to be easy to work with, but you just must work through it because everybody is different. So just pace yourself when it comes to people skills in working with others to maintain strong people skills.

Communication & Listening

As an entrepreneur just like in any other relationship you must have great communication and listening skills. You must be able to communicate well with your team, customers, business partners, etc. A lot of the success we relied on will have to be on how well your communication skills are. In the times we live in now a lot of communication is done with emails and texts but sometimes those things can get misunderstood about what is being said. So as an entrepreneur it is great to always go back to having great communication face-to-face or over the phone speaking to someone. This will eliminate any misunderstanding. When it comes to listening skills, this is also just as important making sure you are getting a clear understanding of what one is saying or what was said. Being able to hear what your team, employees, or business partners, or customers are saying about their needs or concerns helps to give them the sense that you are listening to them. When you are listening, this helps you to find a solution to what is needed. When you are listening, it helps you to evaluate and help you grow your business. When you are not listening, you may miss out on particularly important information that is given. According to an article, I read it stated that only 10% of us listen effectively. The reason this why is that although we may be listening most of us our mind is somewhere else. How many times have you been somewhere listening to someone speak but your mind and thoughts were somewhere else? It happens to a lot of us. LOL. However, if you do not have the best listening skills now you can get better at your listening skills, so do not let this stop you from being an entrepreneur just work on it.

Patience with others

Having a sense of patience as an entrepreneur is extremely critical to have. Because things will not always come and fall in place the
the way you wanted to as an entrepreneur. You will need patience in the time when you first start as an entrepreneur. Clients, customers, and money will all come in due time so you will have to be patient, continue to put in the work, and keep moving forward. You must first plant the seed and keep watering so that you can see your end results, but all of this still comes with patience. There will be times when you

need to be patient with your customers or your clients and even your team or employees. There will be contracts that you may have to negotiate with and that will come with patience as well. Hey if you think about its life, in general, you must be patient with. We do live in a time where everything is paid for at your convenience. But as we see now in the fourth month of 2020 patience is needed for parents, children, business owners, and more due to the pandemic of Coronavirus. So, if you have not learned patience yet with what we are going through now you would come out learning patience after this crazy pandemic is over. As an entrepreneur, while you are having patience with going through the process of building your business also enjoy the moment of the journey because every small goal accomplished is something to celebrate. So, appreciate the patience.

Knowing your target audience

As you are becoming an entrepreneur, or maybe you are already one, you need to know who your target audience is. One thing that I learned from one of my coaches Taurea Avant, is that one of the biggest mistakes entrepreneurs make is saying that their product or services are for everybody. You must break down specific details of who your target audience is going to be. And then focus on catering and putting your product and services out to that specific target audience. Knowing your target audience is a great marketing strategy for entrepreneurs or business owners. Once you know who your target audience is you will know how to understand and communicate to their needs. There are many ways to market on social media, choosing your specific target audience so you are only getting people that are interested in that product or services you have to offer. Yes, there may be a handful of people that are not in your target audience that may still be interested in your product or services but that is okay. Let your focus be for that specific target audience you have set. If you find that the target market that you have set is not working for you, you can always go and change it to something else. Then start working on that target audience as your new target audience. Again, remember I stated before being an entrepreneur is all trial and error you will find what works best for you and your business. For more valuable information please go to www.cowanostanley.com.

Leadership

Do you consider yourself a leader? Now as an entrepreneur you should have traits of leadership. For instance, if you are a business coach or some type of coach you should have leadership skills. When being a leader you want to be able to give good valuable information and good habits that others can follow. When being a leader you want to be focused on being able to lead people in the right direction. Leadership is one that will spark your growth in your business. Many entrepreneurs miss the importance of having leadership. Being a leader means that you would need to make sure you are looking in and out to resolve solutions and problems. When you an entrepreneur and you are a leader you must know who you are. Leadership comes with all these characteristics and traits that you have read in this book. So, it is a full-time job to be able to carry all of this. Are you ready to be in leadership? Whether you are a leader in your church, in your business, or your job and other positions all these characteristics for leadership are needed. As an entrepreneur having a vision is one that a leader must-have. How can someone follow you if you do not even know where you are going? So, you must have the trait of leadership in order to be able to have others follow you. In leadership, you should be able to help others develop and grow. An effective way of leadership is being able to be supportive of others also. Most of all leadership will consist of having perseverance. When you can start seeing the results of your leadership through other people than you are doing something right.

Conclusion

Now that we have given you many acquire traits and characteristics of a driven entrepreneur; do you think you have what it takes to pursue entrepreneurship. Or maybe you are an entrepreneur that needs to brush up on a few things that you didn't even think about. Whatever the case may be, nothing is impossible to do. Whether you are wanting to be an entrepreneur or a business owner, or an exceptional employee all these traits can be used to better yourself as an individual. We all can make some adjustments and changes to how we handle situations and the behavior we may carry. Sometimes is just the mindset of recognizing what is we need to do and doing it. The fact is that majority of these traits will come with trial and error as you go through life all at different time and stage in life.

If you are a driven person you will do what necessary to find ways to keep pushing along the journey. Enjoy every moment of our journey as you navigate through becoming an entrepreneur or becoming a better entrepreneur in the area that you service. Even myself I continue to practice and make a habit of doing better in all these areas as an entrepreneur. Taking the time to yourself maybe thirty minutes to an hour meditation to reflect on you, will help you each day.

I hope and pray that this book has been a blessing to you in helping you on your journey to acquire these traits as an entrepreneur or business owner. If you have gotten great information from this book please share your testimonial by going to www.cowanostanley.com and submit your information.

About the Author

CoWano Stanley is from El Dorado, AR, but she grew up in Minneapolis, MN. She is the mother of a 20-year-old son. She has completed two undergraduate degrees, and two master's degrees, most recent is a Master of Accounting & Financial Management. She left corporate America in July 2018 to start her own business & entrepreneurial goals. She has self-published two books, "It's Time to Live," in Sept 2017 & "Bet on Yourself" in Feb 2020. She is also a Co-author in two collaboration books called. "From Employee to Entrepreneur and Life of an Entrepreneur."

As a business owner, CoWano knows it takes hard work, dedication, and motivation to makes things happen. CoWano's mission in life is to help inspire and encourage others that they can accomplish any goal or dream they desire and to bet on yourself. She has more goals she wants to achieve still, but it all takes time and patient as well as a process to get to the finish line. No matter how long it takes or the obstacles that you must go through to get there but to never give up, and always believe in yourself. You will have some Wins, and you will have some losses (but losses are not bad they are only lessons or what not to do. However, keep pushing and moving forward, as there is always a light at the end of the tunnel. But most importantly, always keep God first, and he will direct your path along the way.

Follow Ms. CoWano "Coco" Stanley on Social Media

 cowanococostanley

 cowanostanley

 cowanostanley

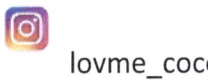 lovme_coco

 startupwomenalliance

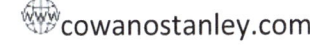 cowanostanley.com

www.ingramcontent.com/pod-product-compliance
Lightning Source LLC
Chambersburg PA
CBHW042333150426
43194CB00001B/41